Customs

CUSTOMS

Poems by Joseph Duemer

The University of Georgia Press
Athens and London

© 1987 by Joseph Duemer
Published by the University of Georgia Press
Athens, Georgia 30602
All rights reserved

Designed by Betty P. McDaniel
Set in Sabon with Stencil Bold display
The paper in this book meets the guidelines for
permanence and durability of the Committee on
Production Guidelines for Book Longevity of the
Council on Library Resources.

Printed in the United States of America

91 90 89 88 87   5 4 3 2 1

Library of Congress Cataloging in Publication Data

Duemer, Joseph.
  Customs.

  I. Title.
PS3554.U3145C8   1987   811'.54   87-13791
ISBN 0-8203-0966-4 (alk. paper)
ISBN 0-8203-0967-2 (pbk. : alk. paper)

British Library Cataloging in Publication Data
available

In memory of my mother, Evelyn Duemer

As I went out on a merry morning,
I heard a bird both weep and sing.
This was the tenor of her talking:
Timor mortis conturbat me.

Acknowledgments

I am grateful for a grant from the National Endowment for the Arts which enabled me to work on many of these poems during 1984. I am also grateful to the National Endowment for the Humanities for a grant that allowed time to think, write, and study literature during the summer of 1985.

"Waves," originally published in *Tar River Poetry,* was reprinted in *The Anthology of Magazine Verse and Yearbook of American Poetry* (Monitor Book Company, 1985). "Seeing the Farm," originally published in *Porch,* was reprinted in *Rain in the Forest, Light in the Trees: Contemporary Poetry from the Northwest* (Owl Creek Press, 1983).

"The Gazelles" was included in *Fool's Paradise,* a chapbook published by the Charles Street Press (Baltimore) in 1980. "Waves," "Letter from the Field of Play," and "Fireworks" were included in *The Light of Common Day,* a chapbook published by the Windhover Press (Iowa City) in 1986.

Acknowledgment is made to the following publications for poems that originally appeared in them. Some of the poems have been revised since their first publication.

The Antioch Review: "Four Flat Songs"
Arete: The Journal of Sport Literature: "Night Baseball in the American West"
AWP Newsletter: "Origins of the English Language"
The Hollins Critic: "Supplication"
The Iowa Review: "Three for Mike Cummings"
Jeopardy: "Timor Mortis"
The Mid-American Review: "Songs I Could Sing You," "Letter Home," "Streambed"
Montana Review: "Telephone"
MSS: "Burn Victim," "The Loveliness of Two Retarded Girls Eating Lunch," "Recidivist's Song," "That's What Friends Are For"
Poetry Northwest: "The Gazelles," "The Second Person as Muse"
Porch: "Two Notes," "Seeing the Farm"

Scape: "Delmore Schwartz Enters into Heaven"
Seattle Review: "Roofing the Barn"
Tar River Poetry: "Scene," "Waves"
Tendril: "A Quarry in Indiana," "Prayer"
Western Humanities Review: "Old Men Sitting in a Bar"

The book's epigraph is from an anonymous fifteenth-century lyric; the title of "Amateurs in Paradise" is a phrase lifted from E. A. Robinson's poem "Two Gardens in Linndale"; the epigraph of "Songs I Could Sing You" is from Yehuda Amichai's poem "Quick and Bitter," and there is a line of Wallace Stevens's quoted later in the poem. Section 5 of my poem "Sonagrams" owes much to Laurence Lieberman. I would also like to acknowledge Bruce Anderson and Stan Hodson, who both know that what Hannah Arendt said is true: "Poets are the only people to whom love is not only a crucial, but an indispensable experience, which entitles them to mistake it for a universal one."

Contents

Part Four

PART ONE

The Loveliness of Two Retarded Girls
Eating Lunch

Awkward as sailboats
in uncertain wind
they are not beautiful
in any way we'd understand.

There is disorder in the light
welled in their faces
and in their eyes the willed
focus of a sleek bird's gaze.

Intent, they watch their hands
go about their business
with amazement. Reach for them
is a kind of reverence—clumsy

as all holy things. Through
her intellectual's slim smile
one subvocalizes steadily,
as if by whispering to herself

thin syllables of rage,
she might pray the world still.
The other munches
sliced vegetables and an egg

with subtle delicacy not to be
believed by those smart enough
to walk through the deepest gestures
without thinking.

Burn Victim

When I was a dumb boy, this girl
a little older undressed alone
and got in bed before I was allowed
in the dark room, or in under darker

sheets. I was not to see her arms
laced with long scars, and rough
some places, like the silver bark
of sapling elms. But she moved

toward me, softening like fire,
opening like burned wood, and pulled
me safely through the smoldering air
every day for one long summer.

It was hot inside of her, and sweet
as a garden drenched with rain.
We hardly spoke—how could we,
doing each other this distant,

elemental favor? I must have felt
to her, the way, at night, my own heart
feels—reliable, thumping quietly.
It doesn't know what it is doing.

Seeing the Farm

Aristotle had something like this in mind
when he described bodies in motion
as *desiring* their proper locations . . .

A jet, the apparent size of a high crow,
trails two scarves of pink vapor away
from the sunset. Motion

is only the desire to be at rest:
the maul is almost asleep when the log
splits—the moment of failure like being

in love with someone who shares your birthday,
or like being the child riding in a car
who looks up from a book and sees

for the first time a red barn, and who remembers,
miles later, a man standing in front of it,
so still he could almost have been asleep.

Telephone

He remembers the first time distance filled him
with the fear of eternity, the first time as a child
he looked into the sky and tried to think. That day
the clouds were unimaginable animals; their broken forms
filled the sky the way the bodies of buffalo driven
into canyons by Apache hunters filled the canyons.

After she has left him, his wife phones
from out of town. His tears fall in the perfect holes
of the receiver—she hears this as the sound of stones
falling to earth from a great height. But it is their words
gathering in the wires and dying.
                                          He tries anyway
to describe the time he saw birds turning in sunlight—
the way the whole flock darkened at once as it turned.
"It's as if they're sending messages in code."
Holding the phone's black body, he speaks
softly into a distance you cannot shout across.

A Quarry in Indiana

I have left the house of the vague
      friends of a woman
            I love, but not well.
It is late afternoon. The ditches
      by the road to the quarry are riot
            with horsetails, dock, clouds
of midges. Scattered milkweeds
      are dotted with monarch
            butterflies
depositing their eggs in the soft
      stems. Unhinging, they decorate
            the earth like odd leaves.

I am carrying enough beer
      to last
            into evening;
I was embarrassed
      by the seriousness and logic
            of the conversation after lunch.
This isn't the kind of weather
      one takes a casual walk
            in. It requires
a serious desire to be elsewhere.
      The folk who settled here
            must have hated where they came from.
But the best limestone in the world
      is quarried here—
            Bedford stone, the grade
other limestone is judged by.
      Deposited
            by a Silurian ocean,

it has waited for quarrymen
        desperate or crazy
                enough
to see profit in it. This blue-
        gray limestone
                is a crop
and the men who cut it
        from the hills are proud
                as farmers in years of good
                weather.

This quarry, though, has been
        worked out—
                it's a gouge littered with slabs
too odd-shaped or cracked
        to haul off.
                Only a few weeds
waver at the edge
        of the pit. None
                have stepped in,
though someday life will
        gather in this
                depression. Already
a lake is beginning to flower
        in the heart
                of the quarry.

Stepping to the edge
        the heat hits me
                as if I'd pulled open
the door of hell. But the heart
        of the stone remains
                cool. Diamondbacks
as thick as a boy's arm
        whisper
                from shade to sun,

the heat hauling their bodies,
        keeping them perfectly
                tuned as a string
of sure bets
        in a slow world, a world
                of half-wits.

On a slab at the rim,
        my last beer sweating
                beside me,
I am confronted
        by the small
                shells of primitive mollusks
embedded in the limestone matrix,
        perfectly white,
                the size of a man's thumbnail:
it didn't take life long
        to invent masks
                for its soft bodies.
The can, as I lift it to drink,
        leaves a moist ring
                on the rock. The moisture,
I know, has set chemistries
        in motion—rings of atoms
                dancing
and buzzing like mosquitoes,
        mating and swarming.
                One-celled
plants and animals begin
        swimming in circles!
                This knowledge
is as close as I've come
        to what Freud called
                the *oceanic feeling,*
the illusion that the world

might love us
            if we love it.
It is so easy to lie!
            We don't even have to choose it.
            That may be
why we are so often amazed
            by confrontations with
                        the solid world:
In the morning
            fog will fill this
                        valley
and spill into the quarry.
            In the fields will be blue
                        horses and deer . . .
(Last night I woke with my heart
            racing so fast and hard
                        it shook my bed.
Where had I been
            to expend so much
                        energy, to wake
in so much fear?)
            . . . now, with the hopeful insect-din
                        of alcohol
buzzing in my ears,
            I start back. A long way.
                        It is still
hot, but the bushes
            no longer burn with monarchs:
                        The best days
of my childhood
            were this
                        lonely.

Four Flat Songs

1.

The window opening north was one of the apartment's
selling points. A broad prospect, painter's light.
And at night the city a swarm of bright points
brilliantly made across the hill, the ship canal
a crooked arm at its unlit base. Seen from your living
room, ships seem to cut through residential streets,
the canal itself hidden by its docks, warehouses, and vessels
moored in their berths. Masts, cranes, superstructure
are all that's visible above the ragged line of industry.
But tonight the lights dance and smoke, products
of unhealthy work in a city out of whack, its bridges drawn,
traffic helpless. Your mind blinks with the lights, not
in warning, but in terror of the earth's slow waves, the hills
cresting finally in this time, breaking under you, no
distance between you and all the shaken world.

2.

The only girl, the youngest child of moneyed alcoholic
Communists, you early shifted for yourself in that house
intrigued with poetry and music. Your eldest brother played
Chopin on the polished grand as you sat rapt, involved in
flipping through Doré's engravings for *Inferno* (from BOMC),
the pictures that had banned a playmate from your house
and later sent you sneaking off to church to save yourself.
For years the birds sang as if on cue in the backyard,
fireflies stitched the lilac to the shadows, and your parents
held their own against the dilettantes that filled the house.
Then the birds went to the dogs. Your father, Milton, died,

left your mother breathing, boozy, misdiagnosed a paranoid.
What's a child in a family that loves Art? Your brothers
committed your mother and packed you off to live with a
     Christian
aunt, whose prim daughter tried to teach you how to dance.

3.

It's a way to work toward quietness. The half-wit woman
on the bus noisily proclaims her Catholicism this Monday
morning by citing points of doctrine to prove her seatmate,
also retarded and apparently a Protestant, will go to hell.
Outside, tulips knock themselves to pieces against a fence;
the spring wind and the dementia of chill light falling
against taut windows are ways to work toward warmth. Fear
is a great formalist. I'm trying to explain myself. Love,
says Freud, is a better cure than art as we rush toward
pleasure, or at least away from pain. I wince at the logic
of the motto stenciled on the woman's plastic book bag:
OUT TO LUNCH. I'm learning, slowly, that to be cut off is not
necessarily to be a genius. Accept this sublimation
as a gift. Forgive my half-baked promises and silences—
and forgive your own voice rising, making able sense.

4.

On your wedding day it rained like hell. It beat
the last petals from the last roses, soaked your dress.
(That night as you undressed you found bright splotches
on your body where the dye had transferred flowers.)
The justice of the peace's lime living room
was actually adorned with plaster cupids. Christ. Perhaps
the sheer bad taste startled you—at any rate, your contact
lens slipped from the center of your eye and stuck beneath
the lid, where you wore it painfully, ceremoniously into

marriage. The reception was a blind drunk dance. It was still
rainy next morning as the two of you, hung over, left
for a few days in a friend's damp cabin on the beach. . . .
The last day there it finally cleared enough to walk
the shore: along the line of highest tide were clam shells,
perfect holes drilled in their necks by moon snails. They go
straight to the heart, my wife, straight to the heart.

—for M.F.L.

The Second Person as Muse

I was going to begin with *you,* my recalcitrant
Other, empty-hearted, suitable Second Person.
I was going to bring you gracefully into this
story, but you refused me the safety from self-pity
your skirts afford.
                 And I was already
on my knees—though not exactly praying—just looking
out the window at the cops in the parking lot and listening
to the burglar alarm rattling from the back of the florist's.
I was drunk and thought someone was stealing flowers:
I would have, for you. (A car had slipped its brake
and smashed the door.)
                 Even after they got the thing
shut off, I didn't want to sleep. I wanted to ride
with the cops, get a look at better accidents than this
paltry one with no one hurt, no one even in the car.
I wanted to know how it felt to arrive on the scene
with my lights flashing . . . at your house maybe . . .
the squad car filled with armsful of wilting evidence, roses
blinking like neon in the swiveling lights. What I wanted
last night was a shoot-out. . . .
Ah, you would have *danced* through this story.

Two Notes

From Body to Soul:

I hope you're skinnier than I am
or we'll never get through another door,
never again enter the apartments of lovers,
but be forced to stay in the thin cold forever.

From Soul to Body:

I seldom take note of your lumberings—
But near dawn, when you sleep with your lips
parted, I come to the threshold and look closely
at her, at the room. Sometimes I almost call out.

Supplication

Dear God, let me die in my sleep, my poor soul
(in which I still believe, against all evidence)
seeping slowly out through the ends of my hairs
into the warm room. Or let it divide in two and slip
out through the nostrils with my last breath.

For I fear death. I am afraid of heights, and know it
is always a fall from a high place—what has nested
all those years in the head as *consciousness* lets go
and falls clear (by way of the heart, which it quashes,
a hand smothering a candle) to the soles of the feet
and keeps going, punching a hole in the earth.

For entry. Please god may I avoid the public
clutch at the heart as the sidewalk comes up, startled
recognition staring from the faces of pedestrians
into whose day I have offended this mortality.
Nor do I desire like some to die behind the wheel
with a rush hour pulse, taking a passenger and several
home-bound commuters along with me. Yes. In my sleep.

With only those who populate my dreams taking notice—
quiet beasts with half-human faces, cow-eyed,
easily scared and starting off in every direction
at the slightest provocation, banging the surface
of the earth with their hooves. Let my death be so

quiet even these so easily panicked do not startle,
but graze placidly the gray fields of forgetfulness.

The Gazelles

The oldest words are the ones invented for weather.
When there is nothing to say, they gather in the mouth.

I give you a loose gathering of words
like gazelles on the horizon of the savannah.

The antlers of the gazelles glint in the sun,
awkward as love, afraid of themselves.

I give you words, worth nothing, unable to save love
or destroy it, old and broken before I say them.

The gazelle is only a small antelope, noted for grace
and its soft eyes, named after a kind of love poem.

I give you the emptiness of the sky and water.
The gazelles come down the savannah to the water

and their hooves dent the hard earth, leaving
the faint shapes of hearts everywhere.

PART TWO

Nothing Unusual

In the cemetery
I began noticing the way my feet met the plush earth.
We were walking, but not by ourselves.
The earth was full of us
and vast oceans of oxygen poured from the trees,
the grass and the flowering hedge.
An old woman drove by in a Lincoln,
toward some fresh flowers. Some of the markers
were old and wooden, washed clean,
and you know what that means . . .
Yet we were more in love yesterday than before.
How do you explain it?
I have a friend who loves to talk about death.
A happy man, and no alcoholic, his failure is in seeing
only the obvious.
There is no richness like this richness.
No world like this, even the next, which may be dangerous . . .
How do you explain it? Be serious,
this is a graveyard, and over there
is a woman weeping for a man
she slept with forty years.
The next world bears down on us, an axe blade
slamming across
our nervous systems.
But all this oxygen, my friend, is a supply of kisses—
not limitless, but very large—like the joy
I have in touching your hand, or in writing
this conventional poem.

Old Men Sitting in a Bar

Their softened faces glow above the sagging
draperies of washed-gray white shirts.
The pure products of America sit quietly,
fingers wrapped around warm yellow beers:
A small black plastic radio patched with tape
broadcasts a ball game, each inning a bracket
to hang some talk on, though mostly this
room is as quiet and shadowed as the flattened
patterns of a Depression-era photograph.

Prayer

I don't want to
know what is reasonable
when the world is so
persistently unreasonable

It is enough to be present
in the world of appearances
It is enough to know
suffering is both the cure
and cause of love

Trying to be seated
on the bus a blind woman
walks full-force into one of those
steel posts
the impact of her face
cheekbone and forehead
make a sound
like the sound of an axe
striking a tree trunk

or the sound an owl made
in my mind when it ambushed my headlights
as I drove home so drunk
I didn't even swerve
I swear its claws clicked lightly
against the windshield
and then it was gone

She sits down not even heavily
with a bruise invisible to her

opening like a hand
not a lover's hand
across her cheek

It is my face that aches
with realization—she must
come up against the world
this way all the time

Well I don't want to know
her world
don't let her bruise my sleep
it is enough to have some entrance
in the world
something to do
something to keep
doing

Amen

Amateurs in Paradise

I am trying to hear the secret ticking that goes
on all the time, everywhere—the ticking

like insect wings along the furred undersides
of leaves, a sound as small as black flies

that click against smudged glass. Out there
in the yard it is a calm summer afternoon,

the garden shifting its shoulders in the light
wind. The blind ticking has nothing to do

with my memories, I wish it did: the friend
from another life broken and almost dead

after smashing drunk into a cement barrier.
The two of us climbed the frozen rock faces

beside a glacier and didn't even know we were
in love, setting the triggers of avalanches

for later in the winter. And in those same
mountains, a girl unfolded in flannel blankets

a small night within the night, and our breath
rose from the ground with the scent of stars,

making the fur stand on the backs of small
animals deep in their burrows. These worlds

of imagination and memory have nothing to do
with the black ticking from newspapers, from

the plastic cases of radios, from the change
tarnishing in the hand of the Sioux brave

who has hitchhiked with his wife all the way
from S. Dakota, nothing to do with the toothless

addict in the bus station demanding cigarettes.
I slump in the plastic t.v. chair and insert

my quarters; clock ticking, I watch the screen
like a man dreaming, like a man blown through

the side of an airplane by a small packet of
explosives smuggled aboard between the breasts

of a *mujahadeen;* I watch like a man with scorched
eyes, and hands fused into ontogenic fins, falling

for miles toward what looks like the vague green
shapes of paradise, but is only this world.

Scene

Three girls with rings
of eyeshadow darkening their looks
have come in and taken possession of
the restaurant where
I am eating lunch.
They all wear blue jackets
and each, also, small
gold, heart-shaped earrings
in ears pink
from the cold and too small
to hear the whirr
of knives being sharpened
behind them
in the warm kitchen.

They remind me of the slow movements
in Bach, of the stems, the sharp
slips of flowers rising
by the millions in commercial fields:
nothing will stop them.

The girls smoke extravagantly,
with broad gestures,
inhaling superior air and exhaling
sighs of world-weariness.
Their cigarettes

are too long for their fingers, but this
doesn't stop them—
they roll their eyes
at poor us, an assortment

of old regulars reading
books and the afternoon
papers. Such girls don't need us.
They make their own news.

Like forced flowers
they burn coolly at the heart.
Bitter juice nettles
their veins
and hardens
into vanity and worse
vices. Soon
they will neglect even those
worlds that are their faces.
They have begun
burning toward the grim
work of women.
They are bored.

They are certain
they are finished.

Three for Mike Cummings

1. *Desire*

When spring came we thawed my car, pulled
nests from the wheel wells and engine
cavity. Then, we took long drives at night
past fields patched with old snow.

Drunk, we crept through towns
so small we didn't see them
until the next morning.
These were places we could only go

after the bars closed, trespassing,
disturbing the sows.
I still don't know what we were doing there.
Trying to love everything, I guess,

with equal prurience.

2. *Intellect*

In the back bedroom of the farmhouse
near Morse, sometimes I could almost
quit thinking, forget the barn leaning
toward itself, its loft sagging

with tons of wet hay left over
from the days when a small place
could make a go of it. I could have stayed
there forever; the barn was almost massive

enough to defeat thought.

3. *Beauty*

I say *thank you* to the bus driver
and start home through this
suburb of retired fishermen.
I've lost your address.

Across the street, a drunk stumbles
from the padded door of Rosy's Bar
and stops traffic. Taking his time
against the light, he makes the other side

then pauses to yank a rose
from a bush in someone's yard
and gets away with it. Surprised,
he tries for two blocks to poke

the stem through his buttonhole.
No needle ever was more difficult to thread
than this, which will mend nothing.
Defeated, he chucks it,

really guilty now.

That's What Friends Are For

As we get older, my friends and I still
look pretty good to each other, some
blessing adjusting the lines at the eyes'
corners, sag of belly, slight downward tilt
of breasts toward new forms of grace
as we begin to point down into the earth
rather than up out of it; but we find ourselves
still able, grave as we are, to love
each other's solidifying outlines.

The size of our souls may increase
even as we begin to shrink into shapes
resembling our parents' shapes.
My friends' young children look bright
as high summer leaves playing in sun,
and watching them, I understand better
my own distance from death.

Yesterday I saw two girls emerge
from their college dorm dressed in colors
that announced as if with blare of trumpets
their arrival on the street,
celebrating the ability to tip the whole
gray afternoon on its ear. I *remember*
that way of walking, but these girls are now
so foreign they may as well be speaking
Hungarian. I can hardly imagine them
undressed, as I can, however, imagine
my friends' wives. Well, we wear

the faint phosphorescence of death
that colors nipples, glans, labia; we
taste more of earth than of water.
We are already putting our roots down.

Night Baseball in the American West

Nothing echoes against the line
of blue hills except the announcer's
voice, wiry through the p.a. system
as a coyote's drawn out twang.
It isn't much, these
dangled words, announcements—
it's all, the only game in a town
where local teams don't win,
where *visitors* beat the living
daylights out of downtown
streets with those big tires
made for rolling over dunes
like ripples on the surface
of a puddle, ripples on the scarred
surface of the earth, naturally
mute, which speaks only in stories
told by primitives across
a fire's sharp tongues;
but there are no primitives
where everybody wants big trucks,
bright chrome freckled with mud,
instead of the milky inside
of a girlfriend's thigh. Cleats
print the dirt around home plate
with a kind of braille no girl's
hands hurt enough to understand.
The girl is only something
to put up there in the cab.
Now even losers get to play
in sodium vapor light that makes

the whole field look like
a television show. Wives
of the older players sit out
in the parking lot nursing
cold beers, long cigarettes,
black eyes, infants
whose keen howls turn pink
souls green even as some radio
preacher croons sweet Jesus
softly through the dark interior
and the windows start to fog,
turning the right field lights
to quiet fireworks. Far away,
the announcer tells who's next to bat,
and we mistake this for a ritual
when it's nothing but a dance,
when all we know is the score.

—*for Richard Hugo*

Professor of Romance Languages

On a hot night in Indiana, when a crime against
appearance could get you killed, he invited a carnival girl
abandoned by her barker to take his bed, while he
made his with a quilt on the kitchen floor.
For which he was dismissed from the podunk college
where even now the same big elms as then shift
in that hot breeze that never seems to go away
in Indiana.
The girl found a ride north soon enough, kept
touring the Midwest, working the booths, a shade sorrier
each night, but not enough so you'd notice, or care
if you did.
The way things were,
she kept going down like a stuffed toy, softly: falling
for one local after another because they lived somewhere.
They'd have a drink from his bottle and let his hands
drift under her blouse, where the work she did
on warm nights
made the skin slick at the small of her back,
and in the secret crescents beneath her breasts.
Then he'd lay
her down among the rattling bars of a cornfield, settling
into a furrow, her eyes open and blank as the irised disk
floating like a saint's halo above the world.
She hummed a little air,
music of her fears, as he squeezed his eyes closed hard
and made the same round vowel over and over.
A car slid by, lights jarring the tips of the stalks,
but all she could hear was the crickets ripping away
to beat hell.
Years later, she heard he'd gone crazy, was locked up

somewhere for giving aid and comfort to somebody.
He'd never laid a hand on her, just listened to her breathe,
never tried anything—and she'd cut a hell of figure,
she knew. Could have had any man she desired.

Delmore Schwartz Enters into Heaven

Alone at last, and dry, having passed
his forty-fifth year, every inch of him
a pain, having angered, raged, and lied,
he left the world alone.
Little did he know. But he understood
The Cantos, The Bridge, and *Finnegan;*
he used hysteria as best he could.
He broke his own heart.
It was the last mug in the house.
He left his farfetched life, his body
unclaimed, and entered heaven
(the last place that would have him) unsilent
and began to teach the angels Freud
and how many to a pin.

Timor Mortis

Yet the earth contains
The horse as a remembrancer of wild
Arenas we avoid.
—JAMES WRIGHT

Even as a kid dragged against my will
to an old woman's funeral to teach me some dark truth,
I hated grief. I could feel
the heaving and weeping of the thick
lilies, ranks of ladies.

It opens like a slack door
in a river and inside is that dead friend
of my mother's—that object, that lesson—waiting with kisses
worse than the pure anger of horses.

The inside of the river
must writhe with the terrified muscles of horses. I hope for him
it was like falling asleep by a woman
gentle with horses, a woman with no use for the next world,
being graceful in this one.

PART THREE

Recidivist's Song

The woman who signed me up for health
insurance sang out as I was leaving her office,
"I hope you never need it!"

Could I have nodded affirmation smiling,
only to reveal my teeth crumbling into gray
calculus even as I said *good-bye*?

How could I have told her
that I'd come to this
from years of taking my own medicine?

That I have an incurable desire
to make my stories come out right,
even if it means a whole day shot

sitting with my elbows on a sticky bar
working up the perfect explanation
for a wrong? Each new diagnosis

focuses what I most fear that day.
And makes me want to drink and drink,
tilting back my light head on my neck

like a bird at a sunlit puddle.

Songs I Could Sing You

Slow and sweet were the nights
When my hands did not touch one another in despair
But with the love of your body
Which came between them.

—Yehuda Amichai

Through a crack in the door, Gorky
　　told a casual art-lover
　　　　who wanted to chat,
"You must be out of your mind."
　　Professor Luba told me
　　　　Mozart's best music
was written to pay debts
　　and was performed at a fair
　　　　by a steam-powered "mechanical
orchestra." "Leave it to the Germans,"
　　he said, but I could tell
　　　　he was impressed
and meant for me
　　to be impressed.
　　　　I was.

Here, a crow paces
　　the little circumference
　　　　at the top of a phone pole,
nearly throws itself
　　from the cross-bar barking
　　　　at gulls and leaning into
a hard wind, mad if that's
　　possible for crows, but full
　　　　of joy, at least.

Now, we both have other things to
        tend, but have met here
                on this neutral patch of lawn
to say how things are
        with us. I will not
                speak well.
I will not use words to make you
        love me more
                than you already love me
now. As if words could.
        I am sad today
                not because I love you,
but because I love you
        yet resort to words
                instead of silence.

I woke last night amazed
        you slept beside me.
                I touched the plane
between your shoulders
        and felt your muscles tense,
                relax.
Now I've begun believing
        there is only disorder
                between men and women.
But joy shook
        through me
                one night.

When my friend Leland, a painter,
        says *colors* he means
                pigments—
and the possibility of a transformation
        into pigments . . .

                I remember picking
apples with our friends
        in drenching rain:
                huge horses swayed
toward us across their pasture,
        and those horses—in the right song—might
                have stood for something
as solidly as they stood
        on the ground
                crunching windfall apples
from our hands.
        Might have helped grace
                and beauty split the hard
differences that even then
        kept our hearts
                socked in. The apples
that day were . . . what? Dusky? Muted?
        This: You could see
                the blue in them, of distance.
The apples filled twelve boxes
        and what we could not carry off
                we fed the horses, glad
to have finally discovered why
        we had been picking
                apples.

"No possom, no sop, no taters," dear
        and nothing either
                to make music
or fall silent with
        but our voices, worse
                for wear than the crow's.
It's all in the gestures:
        you don't have to know German
                to know *The Magic Flute*

is funny.
　　　　Even on the radio.
　　　　　　Walking

this morning in the field
　　　　behind my house, I found
　　　　　　two old cars, hulks,
and cut my knee
　　　　stumbling into what was left of
　　　　　　an old tractor.
Sparrows
　　　　sang in the empty silo
　　　　　　and a cardinal threatened
from a hollow elm,
　　　　each note an atom
　　　　　　(more empty space than matter),
words spoken over
　　　　the lip of a deep well.
　　　　　　I love this
countryside
　　　　but hardly live here.
　　　　　　To name what can be touched
is madness, but a kind
　　　　we're good at.
　　　　　　I won't wake
like this again, surrounded
　　　　by the safety of your
　　　　　　voice.

Letter from the Field of Play

The clouds here, Frannie, are as real as the great
    splotched quick lumbering sows
        we saw in Iowa:
Ice-light milk-light marble-light, the clouds here
    pile—some days *slam*—against
        the Cascade Range
    Glory be to God for splotched things.

The light this afternoon flattens houses, but sings
    in the foliage until it trembles.
        The play field
In the middle distance simmers with boys fielding bodies
    entranced by supple laws
        of motion:
Green light so deep you might think you could fall into it.
    Knowledge is loved information. This
        afternoon, everything
I know about the way long shadows take the field
    one blade at a time is yours
        for the asking.

Remember the cold Thanksgiving day we walked with friends
    past beat-up farmyards and sagging
        pens to a tilting
Cemetery: fenced like the other fields, but no more
    serious. Sleet stung the stones
        that marked,
Some of them, lives shorter than ours, and stuck. Those
    fields we walked past, heads down
        against the wind,

Only *looked* empty. Generations of harvests slept in them—
    all around us gold kernels with hair
        triggers nestled and
        clicked in the bins.

Lately, Frannie, I have been unreasonably happy. And
    this morning I was awakened
        by tufts of shadow
Wheeling across my walls and bedspread: the cottonwoods
    at the foot of the pasture had ripened
        and were releasing
Wave after wave of their seeds to the havoc of the wind.
    The air was full, and has remained
        full all day.

Roofing the Barn

Whidbey Island, Washington

Through waves of heat, black cattle at the far
end of the field cast shadows black as pits in the earth.
Starting seven feet up, near an outer wall, I worked toward
the ridge, prying out nails, letting fall
rotten shingles spongy with generations of bugs and moss,

until, perched out in the air, a sack of imbalanced bones
swinging a hammer, I had to inch down backward for a beer
and spend the rest of the day on solid ground sending up tools
and lumber for braces on a rope slung over a beam. Eric's kid
   brother,
going into the Navy next day, full of bravado, walked

over the old timbers, casting a shadow fifty feet into the field.
By evening, the roof laid open; we gazed
through it at clouds glowing in long twilight over
a fringe of pine and hemlock on a western ridge. Barn swallows,
virtuoso pilots, slipped and jittered around the open frame.

In summer that kind of light can last halfway till midnight,
so we ate dinner on the porch, facing our work; hands stiffening
around our forks we shoveled in beef raised in the field before
our eyes. Then Eric, who loves anything that flies, began
flipping a glow-in-the-dark frisbee in the air and catching it:

slowly, front chair legs coming to rest gently on earth, we
   drifted
into the night so far we were ghosts to each other.

But between our hands grew long arcs of phosphorescence as
    white
as starlight: over and over, back and forth, until we had woven
over our heads a roof of light vibrant with shouts of joy.

Streambed

William Blake knew something about the eye
and discovered love
in *desarts*. He looked through the world
as we look through the water of this
stream pouring from Palm Canyon's pink mouth
so utterly clear it causes the pebbles
and flakes of mica
to glow violently, as if with love.
There's no one else in the park
to witness this sport and mystery.
Last night the full moon filled
the mouth of the canyon with milk.
No, we can never be innocent, we know
the minerals' atomic numbers, names of birds.
And last night we rocked the aging camper,
till the soft shocks squeaked like quail.

Small blue-bellied lizards as sharp
as chips of flint, tense their claws
into the grain of rocks
as we slip from the slow shimmer of air into
the quick shimmer of the stream
where we are lighter
and there is the sensation of being
lifted slightly and moved along
slowly with everything else.
We scoop up hands full of coarse sand laced
with little panes of pyrite, fool's gold.
I begin to understand
the water pulsing across our skin began
last year as snow in the mountains.

Your breasts grace this stream like sleepy fish.
When I slip my tongue into you,
it will discover little illuminated windows
of that fool's gold through which Blake
might have seen his way clear
into that other world,
but which I am only able to crush
between my teeth
as I bear into you
and as you bear yourself like water
and we stay moving right where we are.

Letter Home

When I get home I'll tell you that
the bed I slept all summer on
wasn't any good—it didn't have
you in it. In mid-afternoon, then
I'll want to go to bed, and later
will try to tell you something
of the color of the maples
fat with high summer
above the party yesterday
and the sound of the plumped leaves
sliding against each other's surfaces
in the wind before the storm,
as the insouciant children
of my colleagues hopped around
the patio, their skin electrified
by tumbling atoms flung this way
from clear across the cosmos, to make
these kids shed light.
   It hurts to think that
the remainder of my life is
filled with projects of description
and elaboration, but when I get home
we ought anyway to claim
the privilege of parenthesis
and stay in bed longer than
is sensible, giving sensation its due,
where we know the way from one place
to the next without a map,
and what it means to go there,
proceeding in good time.
   So what if it ain't transcendent?

There will at least be time enough
to get back down to business come
to hand—I'll steer my tongue along
the giddy contours of your round
breasts, down through all the s-curves
of sex, and try to feel my way
back along our nerves to the first
time I knew I had a body:
a little boy staring at himself
through flickering transparencies
of bathtub water filled suddenly
with white-hot light. Because,
having lost our innocence, the weird
originality of sexual love is what
lets us—by thinking with our hands
and tongues, that we may be
graced sufficiently with time
and space to contemplate, beneath
sheets of private light, both pieces
and the whole—touch the earth at all.
    You will quell the Rational
by whispering flamboyant French,
which I don't understand,
at the rafters of my back; the studs
in our walls will set up
a subtle racket, fibrillating
the fractured coast of California,
and we'll spend whole minutes
tumbling on the tumbling earth.

Dogs at Dog Beach

1.

My dog has found some other dogs to romp
with, one a muscled, bow-legged dalmation,
the other, several sorts of spaniel leaping
in one mottled body. From where I stand

the waves are distant, tide out but moving
up the reach of gray-brown sand slicked
with light that's almost oily, sun a hot
pink smudge on the horizon. What makes

this a scene? This is where the slow river
comes down, after its confinement between
dikes through the environs of the city, to
the sea. Estuaries are always mysteries.

2.

A dog never swims twice through the same
afternoon. Surge after surge of ocean
pushes up river, and I am wet to my knees
with all the evidence I need that Earth

spins in an establishment of certain forces
that separate the firmament from shifting sand.
Out along the surf line the three dogs cut
a long arc, breakneck, then plunge into

the noise of hissing foam, breasting the waves
that, petered out, wash against my legs
where I stand, a little in the river, swirls
of backwash flattening into dusk around me.

3.

It turns out the dalmatian is stone deaf.
Its owners, a young couple with a baby,
tell me it is cued to things it cannot hear
by following the spaniel's eyes. The girl strips

to a bathing suit and walks into the river;
lying back into the movement of the tide,
she backstrokes toward the bigger breakers
uncoiling silently out there. As she swims

she calls the dogs, thrashing the water, and
they come bounding, all three, raising silver
plumes with their forelegs, concerned, or just
going along to please themselves, and us.

4.

The dogs emerge, tails dripping, and shake,
starting with their tails, themselves. They trot
along the bank as the girl rises from the water
and moves toward us, dragging her hands lightly

across the inky surface. She's still fat
from pregnancy, and the mystery of this
image—slashed pink wakes of light trailing
from her fingers—cannot be taken lightly.

Dogs are this world's great innocents, they understand
not irony, are color-blind; at dusk the ocean silvers
into shades of gray—we start home together,
trotting through the features of a simple universe.

Fireworks

Though we can't hear the brass or strings
from where we live across the bay, inside
our house deep thuds ring the floors
at night when the Civic Philharmonic finishes

its summer program of patriotic numbers
and famous movie scores with brassy flights
of pyrotechnics (once an art unto themselves,
now used to supplement thin work

in less explosive media). Warm nights when
our windows rattle, arm-in-arm we step
outdoors to see the show, bare soles pressed
against cool salty sidewalk: each flowering

colored light is followed moments after blooming
by a shudder that comes up through our feet.
Tonight, sweet luck, the fireworks caught us
deep in one another's arms, practicing the only

art with no media at all. We weren't about
to pull the curtain back for any paltry bursts
offered by the city fathers—too late
for pleasures common to the outer world.

The hum of music tunes our nerves and pulls
one big orchestral note out of thin air.
We pitch perfectly as boats resting in dark berths,
waves of faint applause drifting in across the bay.

Ocean View

Half-way along the public fishing pier, out of
the wind in an elbow of splintered railing,
an old woman teases with hands the color of wet wood
wisps of her invisible white hair. Girls in outsized

shirts covering their damp swimsuits lean way out over
railings hatched with pocketknifed initials
to see big rollers break around the concrete pilings
that sway slightly in the swell. Untanned crescents

cup their skinny butts, and sailors out on liberty
pull sweating half-cases from the backseat of their Charger,
offering the wet cans to the girls, who jostle
and adjust their suits, slipping fingers tipped

with chipped pink polish beneath the tight elastic
bands where beach sand has accumulated all day
like grains of sugar. We all crane our necks to see
what sorts of things flop in the buckets of the fishermen:

Flounder and red crabs, eyes black as beads of iron,
knock against the curved white walls of polystyrene pails;
in plastic bags plopped on the splintered boards, bait fish
shine as coldly as chrome-plated knives.

Humped in her blanket smoking a long cigarette awkwardly
as a girl, the old woman inhales seriously, steadily
as a rocking boat in a dark berth. She tilts
her head a little to one side to hear the perplexing notes

of music swim just beneath the surface of the air to her,
fish from the big brass horns of the invisible orchestra

across the bay just now finishing its program of movie hits
and patriotic numbers with a big display of fireworks.

The crowd along the railing whoops approval as light
from the explosions makes the smoking woman's hair a halo
which all lights gather when the air is thick.
She sees the stars come whooping down in numbers

not to be believed. Like angels with their robes blown
back and streams of bright magnetic hair that burns
and burns until the hearts of atoms glow and golden
metal pours down from heaven over everything.

Waves

Our voices carry some raw sense even when
we can't make out the syllables:
last night as we made love
a neighbor calling out what sounded like a name.

An engine gunned and tires burned
out of a drive across the street.
A dog howled and howled to a blank door
and I couldn't sleep remembering the cold

grip of the Pacific's glass-blue breakers,
glittering surf concealing riptide.
I lay awake listening hard
to your breath come and go, afraid again

because I couldn't help you in the waves
or later, while we tried to sleep
through fits and starts of music, the radio
left playing because we were scared

of the white noise hissing in our ears.
When surf has worn you down you can't hear
anything but your own heart and lungs
revving helplessly. So, heart, let's swim

into each other's bodies, noisy oceans
where it's possible to drown in that light
beneath the threshold of the visible
pouring in slow waves from our saved skins.

PART FOUR

Origins of the English Language

My language is originating before my eyes, in the mouth
of this woman who spent a rainy season building
a raft, lashing sticks and stolen lumber so that she
might escape with her family. Had she been discovered
soldiers would have chopped her with carbine fire
and let the pieces curve away along the slow current.

She will not open her hands cupped over the current
set of exercises, where she translates words from my mouth
into crossed, black characters, sticks supporting fire.
It occurs to me how utterly safe we are in this building
where I sit behind a sturdy laboratory table covered
with fire resistant material. It may be that she

can only see the table's legs as sticks, something she
could burn, or grab in breakers near rocks where currents
had persuaded her. She is afraid of being discovered
at large, this student of a new regime, her grim mouth
compressed as the horizon. Today, we are building
a grammar, a law, she thinks; my words are an approaching fire

so that she hunches over, sheltering them, as if the fire
were her sentences. Even in her despair she
makes enough light to float her thoughts—building
again, with her own hands, in secret, for hard currents.
I go back and sit at my bench, unable to open my mouth
for fear of flames and shadowy water. She has discovered

an ally who respects substance; the most serious discoveries
are made stubbornly in silence. As I drive home, brush fires
flicker in the tall grass of the median, and I mouth

songs burned into the language by radio repetition. She's
home now too, I think, in a steamy kitchen where currents
of Vietnamese have carried her. I watch as a building

up ahead sprouts flames as if bombed, and then the building
is gone. The radio reports some scientists have almost
   discovered
"the ultimate nature of the universe." It's a current,
they say. Here in California everything comes to water and fire,
and while we fumble tenses, lose track of antecedents, she
and I, we keep this tongue-tied spirit burning in our mouths.

In the Old City

Barcelona, after Ponc Pons

This gray street has always had these bars with girls
lined up along them talking secretly among themselves,
their elbows folded back like wings dipped in thin pools
of wine, shoulders modeled by blue neon, shadows

curved like blunt fingers around the bones of their faces.
Two American boys are pushing wadded pesetas
at the breasts of one of the whores, who is
laughing; the old paving stones sway under me like heavy waves

washing into the harbor and lapping against blind hulls.
I don't know the languages of smoke and curtains
the girls speak to each other, these dancers
and superb technicians who turn the noise from jukeboxes

into the whispered music of nylon stockings—
though none of them is beautiful. The pretty ones
don't come to this, to be the dangerous children of knives
sharpened against the grit of buckled sidewalks

in the old city of that great anatomist Picasso, whose hands
knew how to use them. From stone doorways
beneath jittery signs in my own language, their eyes
follow me along the street; overhead, iron balconies

rise like ladders—if only I could climb into those rooms!
Or stumble through an old doorway lit by stars
into a courtyard with a fountain where the girls
rinse their long black hair in water that reflects their eyes.

Sons of the Etruscans

Fisole

We climbed up past the monument to local policemen killed
        by Nazis, the air green
with distance above the far city and filled with brilliant finches.
        We hadn't known
which stop to ask for on the bus from Florence, and my Italian
        failed on the driver who knew,
mysteriously, our plans by heart, grandly gesturing the right
    stop.
        I've never seen more light.

We climbed past the black monument shaped like five huge
    thorns
        to the church of Saint Alexander,
where a man swept shriveled olives from the stones with twigs
        bound together in a broom.
Wind chattered the church's window glass against stone sills
        and furred the cropped grass;
inside, columns as graceful as human arms, each entasis slightly
        different, thrummed

silently in templed air stung by gusts of sunlight from the
    shivering
        blue windows. Etruscans
built here first, gazing *at,* not *through,* the atmosphere; then
    Romans
        (temple to a minor god),
then Ostrogoths turned Christians—all looking to turn the
    invisible
        inside out—make it give

itself away for good. But only monks can take this wind for
    long,
            the way it mixes with light.

Up further, at the summit, the Monastery of Saint Francis,
    giftshop
            locked this time of year:
only a pilgrim in high-heeled cowboy boots and rayon shirt
    dozing
            on a pew, skinny white
candles burning slowly down around the little church, lighting
            rows of smudgy saints displayed
on blistered canvas, nineteenth-century restorations peeling
            back like fungused bark.

Outside, in windy light we gazed through the gate at roses
    growing
            in the cloister where
Bernardino of Siena tried to stare away earth's fabric, but found
            too much to love.
I slipped 1000 L to Saint Francis, picking up a printed prayer
            as we turned (quietly,
so as not to wake the gaudy pilgrim) to walk back down the hill
            and catch our bus.

But as if a door had opened in the air, a door opened and a
    priest
            in black silk cassock stopped us,
arms lifted up in welcome making black wings that rattled in
    the wind
            like sails. *Il Museo, vieni!*
We were ushered down a flight of stairs into a dusty limbo for
    lost
            objects, a daylight basement (through

67

high windows we could see the waving tops of trees) floored
        with slabs of rock and lined

floor to ceiling with archeological junk—along with local
    stuff—
            the old priest had collected
on missionary trips to Egypt, China, and the States: row on row
        of Chinese and Roman coins,
glazed chunks of crockery (the size and shape of sharks' teeth)
    from
            half-a-dozen civilizations;
ten shelves of impassive gilded bronze incense-blackened ivory
    and
            painted wooden Buddhas; one

whole room devoted to the pastel civilization of the gay, death-
    loving
            Etruscans. Our reflections
(softened by a furry layer of dust) looked out at us from cases
    jammed
            with forlorn artifacts,
the dim outlines of our heads as indistinct as an obscure caesar's
    image
            sunk in scabby bronze.
The sorts of coins, we're told, that work up from the hillside's
    soil
            like shrapnel from a wound.

Now the priest conducts us to the dimmest, farthest basement
    room, where
            sleeps the pride of his museum—
a ragged and unravelling mummy, some poor unsuspecting
    Middle Kingdom
            middle management official

with the bad luck to die, x-rays might show, of a broken leg
        improperly
                set, a gray fog of infection
blurring the image on the film—in contrast to the oval stone
                wrapped against his breast

where his soul, out of the wind, must rest. That's all there is.
                We pause, about to go . . .
"This wall," our guide says, reaching out, "was built by the
        Etruscans."
                We touch it. The hewn rocks,
dirt-brown, are big as prince's coffins—who knows how far
        down
                into the earth they go?
Before leading us upstairs, he lays one hand across his chest,
        says,
                "We are sons of the Etruscans!"

At stair-top, one last marvel, a modern Madonna in the Chinese
        manner,
                like something they might sell
to tourists in some cheap Stateside Chinatown, framed in
        lacquered black
                bamboo. Painted on her
sky-blue robes, a bright red sacred heart glows between her
        breasts—
                a cartoon light bulb
shooting little rays of light. Beneath her feet there is a shrine
                to Chinese Catholics "killed by Mao."

Our guide stops here praying briefly in fluent Mandarin, then
        releases
                us back into the hum of time.
Everything downhill from where we stand, we stagger out like
        drunks,

                    or blind ones
just returned to light, through stands of those drab Tuscan
    cypresses
                    you see out of square windows
in paintings from the early Renaissance—a device used to
    indicate
                    the presence of a larger world

outside, in which man moves by special grace. We catch our
    breath
                    aboard the Florence bus,
our hands—mine over yours—wrapped around the brushed
    steel columns
                    to balance us through
one hard curve after another. The driver hums a pop tune as
    sincerely
                    as a prayer, and we watch the light
chatter against the rattling blue squares of safety glass, finches
                    scattering through the roadside branches.

Poem at Dusk

From the train all afternoon we watched landscape
flicker through a whir of trees so that now
this small green park with a pool
set in the ground for ducks seems to move

beneath our feet. Trellised roses hover
over the low wire cages of exotic fowl—
one big golden pheasant cock struts neurotically
across his patch of earth, swept clean by a

fantastic four-foot tail, where his spurred feet
leave star-shaped scars. Six spotted deer stare
through a chainlink fence at us, the buck's
antlers tilting oddly, projecting architectures

of shadow we would live in like a language
if we could. It is best to travel for no reason.
Beyond the duck pond, behind a low fence,
an old mule, fur dull as ashes, stands knee-deep

in a field as green as blood is red. We think
he smiles, softly lapping chunks of apple from
our hands and crunching them resoundingly in boxy
jaws. His klaxon cry of thanks wobbles the evening,

setting the air in motion against the undersides
of leaves. Enduring the quiet that follows,
we wade back through the wide pools gathering
beneath the trees, happy to be somewhere at last.

Customs

As he rifles my shirts and pencils, the customs
guard's black pistol flaps from his hip,
a fat, bruised ear. His assistant, troubling
even in this terrific heat to maintain a look

of casual authority, kicks the butts of hungry-looking
black-eyed kids trying to sneak across the border
into Spain, sending them sprawling or
just raising puffs of dust taking

to their heels, and as the day slows down
my backpack proceeds exploding under
the boss guard's big hands until, finished,
he allows me—with a wave—to be led away

by a taxi driver who negotiates for dirhams
but in Spanish, neither of which add up.
In the backseat of the dented silver-blue Mercedes,
I stare through solid air, the tremendous view

of mountains flung from farmed expanse of valley
floor bigger than anything
I've ever seen. S-curving the mountainside,
I am pressed deep into felt

upholstery as into thick blue dust.
The driver is silent in Spanish and the world outside
the rolled-up windows speaks only raw geology,
subsistence farming, and the perfect system

of communication used by the scraggly goats herded
along the road by children in red plastic rain boots.

A little higher now, I see a knot of bent old women
wrapped in yards of traditional white linen.

They stand beside the road and gaze
through ragged mountain sunlight at their daughters,
wearing Spanish dresses under brightly striped djallabas
and wobbling along the broken shoulder of the mountain

road on flimsy stiletto heels
bought across the border. The first word
I will learn in Arabic is pronounced *shoof,*
shoof—always pronounced twice—*look, look!*

Sonagrams

Chefchaouen, Morocco

1.

Ornithologists have raised broods of sparrows
isolated from their fellows, and from
each other, so that the fledglings cannot
hear specific song, signature of

race and sex. Naturally, the birds sing
badly, wobbling up and down the sparrow
scale without harmonics, overtones dull
as overcast, with no help from the wise old

birds who learned last year to sing.

2.

Now out in *Place Uta el Hamam,* a flock
sputters in inch-deep dust, raising clouds
that drift across the oblong square bathed
in morning sunlight. On our first day

we woke at dawn—here, the moment a black
thread can be told from white—the day's
first call to prayer unspooling
from the mosque, fog-shreds of Koran

pumping through the rattly crystal mikes
of souped-up p.a. systems, and then out of
horn-shaped speakers on the tops of minarets.
Rough at first, long notes smooth as they are

struck by sunlight—the folding and unfolding
wings of songbirds in thin air. Roosters
sprout like flames from every height,
throats throbbing holy dialects of rooster-

prayer. A few boulders high up the mountain
take the light. In the Hotel Andaluz at dawn,
doors unlock on either side of us, and young men
in the courtyard slap ice-cold hotel tapwater

on their faces, whisper prayers in Arabic.

3.

Ayachi's father pulls a meat cart knocked together
from a salvaged Fiat axle, some rough lumber
lashed into a flatbed, and a couple of untwisted
drainpipes, used for thills. The boy, 14,

scratches chickenfeed from TourAfrica groups
to keep himself in Spanish sneakers, Winstons,
and sticky coffee sipped casually at tables
in rickety cafes. He's grown up watching

his father bend double hauling skinned lamb
carcasses up the winding alleys mazing the medina.
He wants to know about America, how much things cost,
but soon takes off, spotting a French couple

more prosperous—*two* cameras, walkman, expensive shoes.

4.

Last night a wedding party trouped beneath
our hotel window, and we leaned out through

the shutters. First came musicians—could
hear them in the distance first—reeling

beneath the window playing reedy snakecharmers'
flutes. Then followed young men arm-in-arm.
Finally the bride led by her sisters: she
walks blind beneath a canopy of cloth-of-gold,

peaked at the center, fringed, extending to
her ankles: She can't see where she is being led!
Embroidered slippers hiss along the broken
concrete alley, stitching the hubbub of celebration

to the mountain silence. This morning children
perch in doorways singing wedding songs as sharply
as the finches people keep, and young men who have danced
all night nod, unemployed at wobbly tables in slant

sunlight, eyeing Western girls in shorts.

5.

Our heads swim in the gleaming atmosphere; no holds
but roots along the steepening trail, we grasp at air.
"Not far!" the boy who guides us shouts—to the ruined
mosque first built by Catholics then shot to hell

when the local Berbers rose. "Come on!" Climbing,
we scatter a little clump of goats as rough and brown
as these hills they scrape to live. (Rich men keep
flocks of sheep.) Even in this wind, the children

watching the goats stand still as shadows of rocks,
only the tails of their man-sized shirts billowing

around their legs and the big collars lifting
as if wings were sprouting from their shoulders.

The view from the crumbling white minaret is famous,
engraved beside the serious young king on every
50-dirham banknote—wages for a week's hard labor.
What can tourists know about the local gods?

Camera out, we take pictures of our guide
and of the one barve goat-child who has followed us
enduring the taunts flung at him in town-Arabic
by the kid in Spanish sneakers who has brought

us to this holy place. Then he takes our picture,
capturing, we see later, the true nature of the place—
dark spirits of the air, sundogs, halos knocked
from saints who couldn't stand the mountain light

or a God as tough as a twisted root.

6.

Glossy crows squat along the warming broken
stones of the Spanish fort. Some people say crows
can be taught to speak, but not these bravos,
wild jinn concocted out of rock

and wind. Acacia, mixed with smoke from braising
meat, thickens the thin air. Three women—
two old, one a skinny girl—go past whispering
in language that might as well be birdsong,

weaving the dark threads of daylight into nets.

Phenomenology of the Gaze

1. *Fès*

A pile of sticky goat skulls
horns still on some of them
half blocks the tannery gate.
A big horse swaybacked with
raw hides shies at the shadow
cast by skulls, hooves
slipping sideways on the domed
wet stones paving the alley.
The boy driving him curses
and smacks hard on the flank
with a lithe stick. That sound
slices through the hammering
of steel hammers from a nearby
street where raw brass is
beaten into plates and bathroom
mirrors for the tourist trade.
Through the gate, a flat arc
of black, hundreds of vats
sunk in the city's hard surface
fester with coloring leathers.
We pay to see this, gagging
at iridescent blue stench rising
from the grounds, tongues turned
to leather in our mouths.
The boy who guides us through
the maze of vats cracks
jokes and laughs but leads us
up to higher ground, where
we can see the miles of cubist-

slanted roofs, minarets
decked out with horn-shaped
p.a. system loudspeakers that
break at noon into a sweat of prayer
cool and deep as the shadows
filling up the gates of mosques,
and the eyes of merchants
standing in a haze of smoke
behind their piles of transistors
scalped from abandoned radios,
or tangerines hauled in on
little mules from the hills
we can see from here
patched with leathery green groves.
Going down
the steps to the tannery floor,
I see in a triangle of shadow
a heap of rags filled with a woman
who sits in mud composed
of pigeon shit, blood,
eight-hundred-year-old dirt—
and it is her job
to pick the tufts of fur from hides
not quite burned clean
soaking for a month in lye.
The rotten fibers will be woven
into shop goods for hippies
doing the medina, and the rest
of us, who get what we expect.
Her hands are flayed red,
legs the swollen white of sheep
skinned and draining in the
Street of Butchers.
The woman looks up from the work
her hands are doing, then pulls

a rag across her face
so as to be unseen and safe
from the air I breathe
and the shadow of hell
that falls from my gaze.

2. *San Diego*

In stucco-colored California,
a great blue heron looms squawking
deeply behind me, then passes over-
head, landing in a field of nettles.
As I walk closer, we turn
our heads toward each other, all eyes.
The bird's breast feathers flow
in the wind as lightly as the ruffling
beards of the old men I saw
removing their shoes
in mosque courtyards in Fès,
long beards lifting slightly
in the breeze that dropped down
over the sizzling rooftops into
the shadows near the gate.
As the old worshipers bend down
to wash their feet in the fountain,
they must catch their own
reflections in the still water
of those round pools.
Beside this river widening
into marsh and sand flats,
I have sometimes seen the whole
sky glowing reflected in a wet reach
of sand, my own image hinged
in a lower corner.
The heron's yellow eyes turn

toward me, twin Jupiters
in the night sky of a desert.
That bird swayed with the nettles,
as gray-blue as overcast, air
between us crackling with chaotic
static. I'm not saying we spoke,
but we gazed hard, making what
phenomenal sense we could of each other.

The Location of My Neighborhood

I must come to terms with these *suburbs,*
with the ugly sociological word as well
as the silly whine of lawnmowers cutting
blond stripes through the damp gray
grass. There was a crazy woman once, lived
down the block, who came by and watched
me push the mower through my clumps and stalks.
"You'd better think about what you're doing,"
she said after a while, with the admonishing
tone and lifted finger of one who might
have been a teacher. The habit of instruction
puts down deep neural roots. I have been
thinking since then about profusion and
the capillary suck of moisture rising
back toward clouds that make no sense, though
any smart-ass weatherman can understand
them. I'd like to put my crazy woman on t.v.—
she could tell them a thing or two about
the weather. Another time, at night in wind
and rain, she asked me, "Do you know where
my home is?" She didn't mean the apartment
down the street where some days she hurled
groceries her son brought out the windows
at the feral cats, who scattered, then
came back to feast. I didn't know, and now
she's moved away, taking her crazy red dog
who growled and lunged even at the hand
that fed. The neighbors say her son,
who every weekend the whole block could hear
cussing out her obstinate stupidity, came

and put her in his car, jammed her in
between his surfboard and her big dirty dog.
   A high school kid now cuts our grass
for pocket money, turning Saturday mornings
into Saturday nights. It was good advice
the crazy lady with the white lopsided face
gave out, and I try to take it, thinking
for instance, how the spongy mat of crabgrass
supports a whole dark universe with laws
stricter than our own. I know myself
well enough to know I claim habitually
the black phoebe, the blue jay, and my
mascot mockingbird as emblems to resolve
the old problems of philosophy and art:
the damaged music of curses flying
through the air and strung like hard black
beads along the wavy line of lawnmower whine;
the clang of a big knife against cement—
the tall man across the backyard fence
is practicing again, his blade refusing to burn
into the air the repetitious anger aching
in his arm. Most of us out here no longer
think hard enough to hear air scrape across
the blades of grass we cultivate—the sound
like ocean whispering in a shell, hiss of waves
and particles in every foreign object, tires
down a wet street at night, a foundation
settling on the brittle bones of television
sets still full of beautiful dry laughter.

Not Native but at Home

Parrots—ten of them, at least—rise from the loquat tree,
their blue-green and red feathers turning into yellow sunlight
the moment I loose the dog across the soaked morning grass.

They have been feeding early, muttering and dropping
shit and hard brown seeds on both sides of the fence that
    separates
my patchy yard from my neighbor's perfect lawn. These feral

escapees come squawking down from the cypress where they
    roost
to bother his retirement. They are that sort of creature, parrots,
and I love them for it. This poor neighborhood would be
    impoverished

if these birds, natives of a country shaped like a tornado,
had not busted the slats of their crates with their wings
and risen like mad toys into the local air, which clearly suits
    them.

I love too that each of them is a bundle of wind-blown currency.
Their beaks curve in a wry smile, almost a sneer—they wear
the look of boys who have pulled a fast one, and who still

have something to show for it. The pet shop owners
will never lure these bravos down from the oceanic branches
of cypress. Even my dog pauses to watch them circle and
    descend

across the street, honoring an orange tree's glossy foliage with
    their

atonal music and the surprising weight of their bodies;
    bouncing,
they eat oranges, juice and dew shimmering on their breast
    feathers.

The Contemporary Poetry Series

Edited by Paul Zimmer

The Contemporary Poetry Series

Edited by Bin Ramke